# THE WISDOM TREE

### a children's story for all ages

### by
### Donna Valentine

Creative House Publishing
www.creativehousepublishing.com

THE WISDOM TREE
A Children's Story for All Ages
by Donna Valentine

Copyright © 2017 by Donna Valentine

All rights reserved including the right of reproduction in whole
or in any part or any form without written permission from the publisher.

Published by
Creative House Publishing
Seattle, Washington
USA
www.creativehousepublishing.com

All photos taken by author on iPhone and cartoonized via BeCasso App
Layout by Ferris Graphic Arts

Valentine, Donna
    THE WISDOM TREE
    A Children's Story for All Ages
    – 1st ed.
    p. cm.
    ISBN: 978-0-9996771-2-4

    www.thewisdomtreestory.com

    1. Children   2. Self-Help   3. Psychology

Printed in United States of America

*This book is lovingly dedicated
to Jude, Ellie and Annaliese.*

On a walk in the forest
I came upon a tree
It was so big and tall
The top was hard to see

The author, Donna Valentine, lives in Seattle, Washington. A retired Air Traffic Controller, she now lives her passion in life through the songs and books she creates.

For more information, please visit:
**www.donna-valentine.com**

*Jude and Ellie Galbraith (Donna's grandchildren),
and their cousin, Annaliese Bachman,
pictured, with the author,
getting knowledge from The Wisdom Tree,
Spring of 2017*

*The message of this book that was for them, is now for us all.*